Shark in the park

Lesley Sims
Adapted from a story by Phil Roxbee Cox
Illustrated by Stephen Cartwright

Designed by Helen Cooke
Edited by Jenny Tyler
Reading consultants: Alison Kelly and Anne Washtell

There is  ery page.

Pup's in the park.
He sees... a shark!

"Look out! A shark! A shark!" Pup barks.

Pup
finds
Fat Cat.

"There's no mistake.
I saw a shark.
It's in the lake!"

"It has a sharp and pointy fin."
"A fin?" mocks Fat Cat, with a grin.

Big Pig is camping in the park.
She's lighting a fire.
Oh, what a spark!

Safe place for fires.
Don't make us shout.
ALWAYS, ALWAYS
PUT THEM OUT!

"Big Pig!
    I've seen a SHARK!"
            Pup barks.

Pig laughs.

You don't see sharks in parks!

Hen's pens are making zig zag marks.
"You won't believe this, Hen!"
Pup barks.

Fat Cat grins.
"You silly Pup!"

And Big Pig grunts,
"He's made it up!"

"A shark," clucks Hen, "has quite a bite."

Sam Sheep still sleeps. He thinks it's night.

"I saw a SHARK, as clear as day!" barks Pup.

I'll show you. Come this way.

Pup takes them all to see the lake.
"Hello! I'm swimming," calls Jake Snake.

He jumps up with a splashy spring.

The 'shark' is Jake Snake's rubber ring!
"Oh dear," says Pup. "I'm a silly thing..."

Puzzles

Puzzle 1
Who is doing what?

sleeping	camping	swimming

Big Pig	Jake Snake	Sam Sheep

Puzzle 2
Who did Pup tell about the shark?
Put the animals in the order Pup found them.

Hen	Sam Sheep	Big Pig	Fat Cat

Puzzle 3
How many things beginning with 'b' can you see?

Puzzle 4
One word is wrong in the speech bubble.
What should it say?

You don't see larks in parks!

Answers to puzzles

Puzzle 1
Who is doing what?

Big Pig	Jake Snake	Sam Sheep

camping	swimming	sleeping

Puzzle 2
Pup found the animals in this order.

1 Fat Cat   2 Big Pig   3 Hen   4 Sam Sheep

Puzzle 3
How many things beginning with 'b' did you see?

boats
bench
bear
bush

balloons
beak
bin

Puzzle 4

About phonics

Phonics is a method of teaching reading used extensively in today's schools. At its heart is an emphasis on identifying the *sounds* of letters, or combinations of letters, that are then put together to make words. These sounds are known as phonemes.

Starting to read

Learning to read is an important milestone for any child. The process can begin well before children start to learn letters and put them together to read words. The sooner children can discover books and enjoy stories and language, the better they will be prepared for reading themselves, first with the help of an adult and then independently.

You can find out more about phonics on the Usborne Very First Reading website, **Usborne.com/veryfirstreading** (US readers go to **www.veryfirstreading.com**). Click on the **Parents** tab at the top of the page, then scroll down and click on **About synthetic phonics**.

Phonemic awareness

An important early stage in pre-reading and early reading is developing phonemic awareness: that is, listening out for the sounds within words. Rhymes, rhyming stories and alliteration are excellent ways of encouraging phonemic awareness.

In this story, your child will soon identify the *a* sound, as in **shark** and **park**. Look out, too, for rhymes such as **fin** – **grin** and **bite** – **night**.

Hearing your child read

If your child is reading a story to you, don't rush to correct mistakes, but be ready to prompt or guide if he or she is struggling. Above all, give plenty of praise and encouragement.

This edition first published in 2020 by Usborne Publishing Ltd., Usborne House, 83-85 Saffron Hill, London EC1N 8RT, England. usborne.com Copyright © 2020, 2006, 2002 Usborne Publishing Ltd.